SHAMAN

PAINTINGS BY
SUSAN
SEDDON
BOULET

A BOOK OF POSTCARDS

Pomegranate Artbooks
San Francisco

Pomegranate Artbooks
Box 6099
Rohnert Park, CA 94927

Pomegranate Europe Ltd.
Fullbridge House, Fullbridge
Maldon, Essex CM9 4LE
England

ISBN 0-7649-0329-2
Pomegranate Catalog No. A885

Pomegranate publishes books of
postcards on a wide range of subjects.
Please write to the publisher for more information.

Designed by Riba Taylor
Printed in Korea
06 05 04 03 02 01   10 9 8 7 6 5 4

To facilitate detachment of the postcards from this book, fold each card along its perforation line before tearing.

SHAMANISM, predating recorded civilization, appears to have arisen with consciousness itself and is, in the broadest sense, a world religion. Its early practice was shared by many indigenous peoples and even today survives in native cultures on all continents.

Shamanic belief in an underworld and an "upper" world, with ordinary reality balanced precariously in between, bears a striking resemblance to Western religion, with its layering of heaven, earth, and hell. Its world of good spirits, guardian spirits, and evil spirits can be compared to the Western litany of archangels, guardian angels, patron saints, and the devil.

In shamanism, all of existence is viewed as highly integrated, and all realities exist simultaneously. Whatever exists has a soul, and therefore all forms are to be recognized and respected. To the shaman falls the task of righting wrongs, appeasing the offended, and repairing the harm caused by humans. To accomplish this, the shaman must journey out of ordinary reality, often with the help of guides and allies who appear in the form of animal spirits.

Words often fail in the attempt to describe shamanic experiences and thus we look to images and symbols that convey something of the mysterious visions that lie just beyond ordinary sight. In Susan Seddon Boulet's work we recognize the reflections of our own inner worlds and secret places, the mythic realms at once personal and universal, past and eternally present. The paintings reproduced here not only celebrate her work but also offer glimpses of ourselves and the possibilities for our existence.

Born in Brazil of British parents in 1941, Boulet grew up in South America and was educated there and in Switzerland. She has delved deep into the essence of myths and folktales from many lands to explore the mystery of inner and outer mythologies—those we form within ourselves and those embedded in our cross-cultural traditions. Now living in the San Francisco Bay Area, Boulet is considered one of today's finest American artists. This book of postcards presents thirty of her exquisite creations.

All of Susan Seddon Boulet's originals reproduced in this book of postcards were rendered using oil pastel, ink, and pencil on artboard.

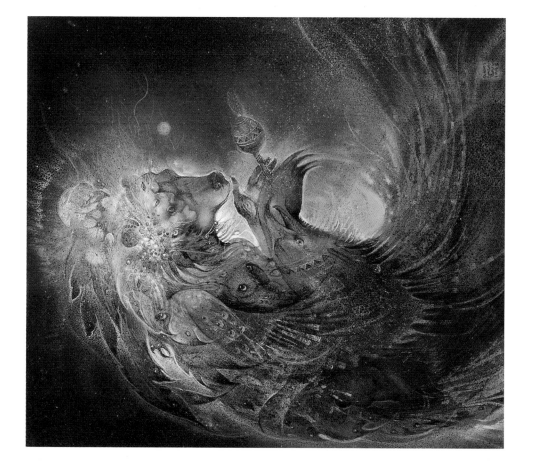

SHAMAN
PAINTINGS BY SUSAN SEDDON BOULET

Bear Woman, 1995

POMEGRANATE BOX 6099 ROHNERT PARK CA 94927

SHAMAN
PAINTINGS BY SUSAN SEDDON BOULET

Midnight Sun, 1983

POMEGRANATE BOX 6099 ROHNERT PARK CA 94927

SHAMAN
PAINTINGS BY SUSAN SEDDON BOULET

The Storytellers, 1992

POMEGRANATE BOX 6099 ROHNERT PARK CA 94927

SHAMAN
PAINTINGS BY SUSAN SEDDON BOULET

Raven Makes Magic, 1993

Pomegranate Box 6099 Rohnert Park CA 94927

SHAMAN
PAINTINGS BY SUSAN SEDDON BOULET

Young Men Shall Have Their Visions, 1982

POMEGRANATE BOX 6099 ROHNERT PARK CA 94927

SHAMAN
PAINTINGS BY SUSAN SEDDON BOULET

The River Gods, 1994

Pomegranate Box 6099 Rohnert Park CA 94927

SHAMAN
PAINTINGS BY SUSAN SEDDON BOULET

Jaguar Brings Fire, 1992

Pomegranate Box 6099 Rohnert Park CA 94927

SHAMAN
PAINTINGS BY SUSAN SEDDON BOULET

Green Voices, 1992

POMEGRANATE BOX 6099 ROHNERT PARK CA 94927

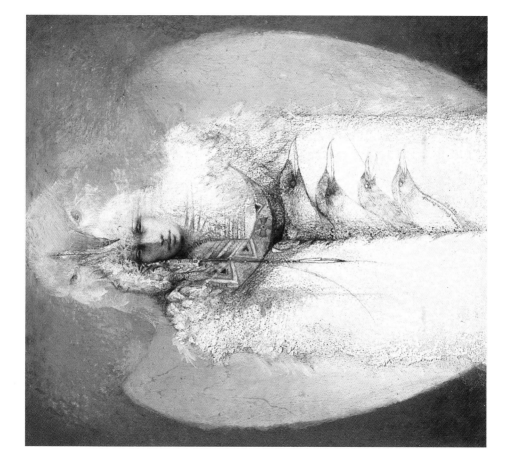

SHAMAN
PAINTINGS BY SUSAN SEDDON BOULET

I Heard the Owl Call My Name, 1982

POMEGRANATE BOX 6099 ROHNERT PARK CA 94927

SHAMAN
PAINTINGS BY SUSAN SEDDON BOULET

Dreamworlds, 1990

POMEGRANATE BOX 6099 ROHNERT PARK CA 94927

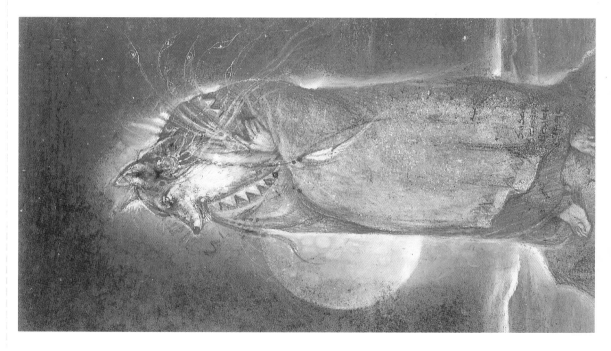

SHAMAN
PAINTINGS BY SUSAN SEDDON BOULET

The Watcher, 1995

POMEGRANATE BOX 6099 ROHNERT PARK CA 94927

SHAMAN
PAINTINGS BY SUSAN SEDDON BOULET

The Birth of Raven, 1993

POMEGRANATE BOX 6099 ROHNERT PARK CA 94927

SHAMAN
PAINTINGS BY SUSAN SEDDON BOULET

Dreaming the Owl Dream, 1989

POMEGRANATE BOX 6099 ROHNERT PARK CA 94927

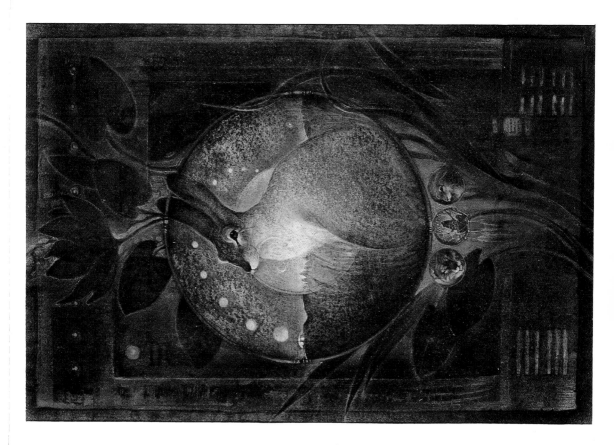

SHAMAN
PAINTINGS BY SUSAN SEDDON BOULET

Kaltes, 1993

POMEGRANATE BOX 6099 ROHNERT PARK CA 94927

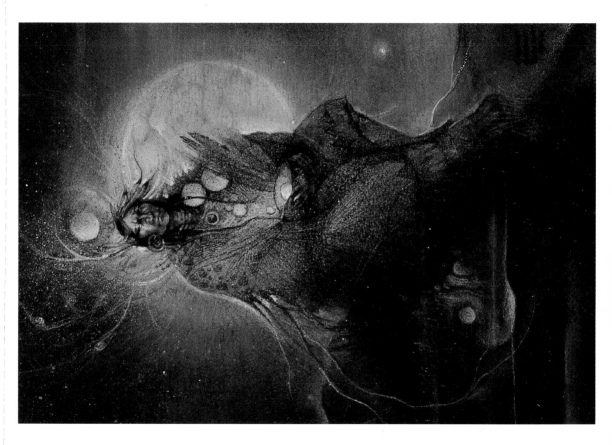

SHAMAN
PAINTINGS BY SUSAN SEDDON BOULET

Medicine Woman, 1994

POMEGRANATE BOX 6099 ROHNERT PARK CA 94927

SHAMAN
PAINTINGS BY SUSAN SEDDON BOULET

Tiger Lily, 1988

POMEGRANATE BOX 6099 ROHNERT PARK CA 94927

SHAMAN
PAINTINGS BY SUSAN SEDDON BOULET

Seven Moons, 1995

POMEGRANATE BOX 6099 ROHNERT PARK CA 94927

SHAMAN
PAINTINGS BY SUSAN SEDDON BOULET

Wolf Wind, 1994

POMEGRANATE BOX 6099 ROHNERT PARK CA 94927

SHAMAN
PAINTINGS BY SUSAN SEDDON BOULET

Lone Wolf, 1993

POMEGRANATE BOX 6099 ROHNERT PARK CA 94927

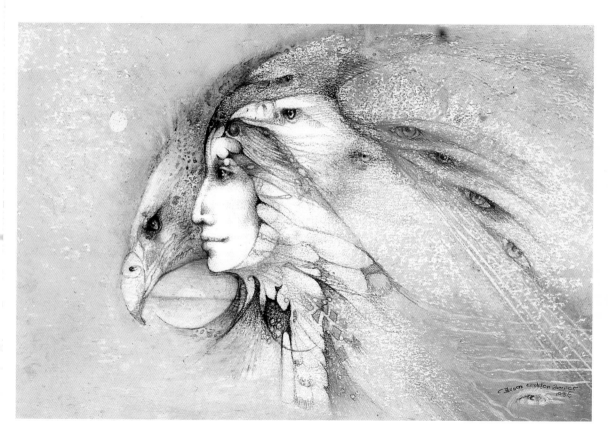

Susan Seddon Boulet
1936

SHAMAN
PAINTINGS BY SUSAN SEDDON BOULET

Eagle Woman, 1986

POMEGRANATE BOX 6099 ROHNERT PARK CA 94927

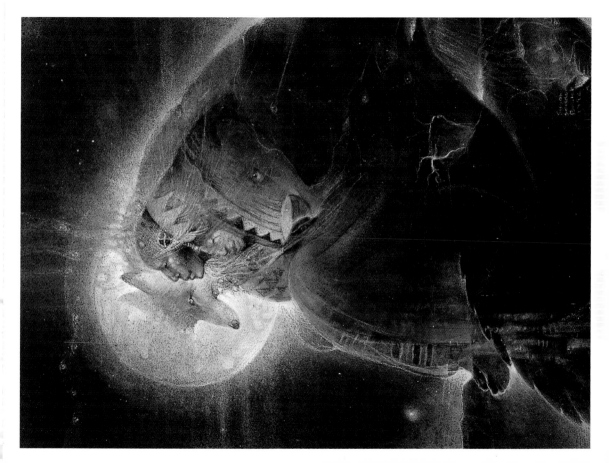

SHAMAN
PAINTINGS BY SUSAN SEDDON BOULET

Vision Quest, 1992

POMEGRANATE BOX 6099 ROHNERT PARK CA 94927

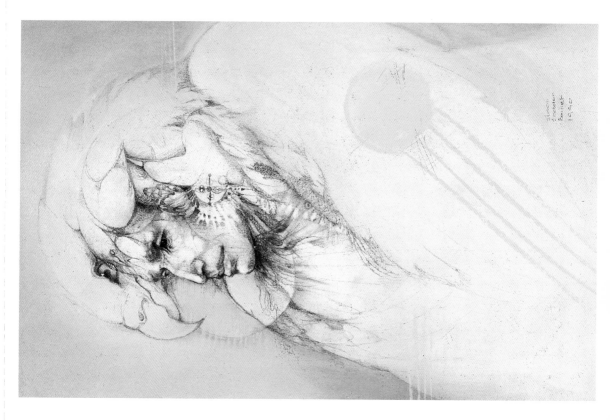

SHAMAN
PAINTINGS BY SUSAN SEDDON BOULET

Father Sky, 1990

POMEGRANATE BOX 6099 ROHNERT PARK CA 94927

SHAMAN
PAINTINGS BY SUSAN SEDDON BOULET

Rites of Passage, 1984

POMEGRANATE BOX 6099 ROHNERT PARK CA 94927

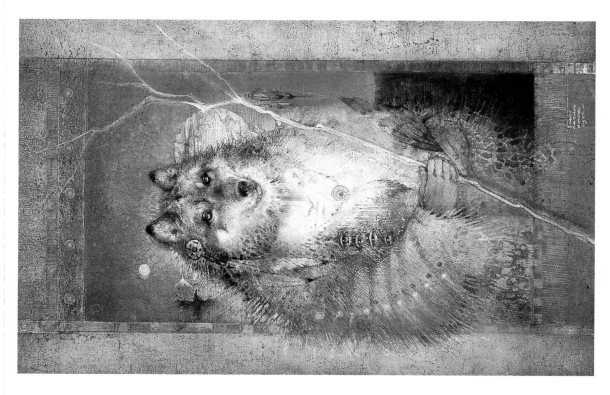

SHAMAN
PAINTINGS BY SUSAN SEDDON BOULET

Grandfather Wolf and His Lightning Stick, 1986

POMEGRANATE BOX 6099 ROHNERT PARK CA 94927

SHAMAN
PAINTINGS BY SUSAN SEDDON BOULET

Companions, 1992

POMEGRANATE BOX 6099 ROHNERT PARK CA 94927

SHAMAN
PAINTINGS BY SUSAN SEDDON BOULET

The Ancient Ones, 1992

POMEGRANATE BOX 6099 ROHNERT PARK CA 94927

SHAMAN
PAINTINGS BY SUSAN SEDDON BOULET

The Navigator, 1993

POMEGRANATE BOX 6099 ROHNERT PARK CA 94927

SHAMAN
PAINTINGS BY SUSAN SEDDON BOULET

Raven's Love of Light, 1993

POMEGRANATE BOX 6099 ROHNERT PARK CA 94927

SHAMAN
PAINTINGS BY SUSAN SEDDON BOULET

Calling the Allies, 1987

POMEGRANATE BOX 6099 ROHNERT PARK CA 94927

SHAMAN
PAINTINGS BY SUSAN SEDDON BOULET

Shaman, 1981

POMEGRANATE BOX 6099 ROHNERT PARK CA 94927